CW00430049

by Iain Gray

Lang**Syne**

PUBLISHING

WRITING *to* REMEMBER

LangSyne
PUBLISHING

WRITING *to* REMEMBER

79 Main Street, Newtongrange,
Midlothian EH22 4NA
Tel: 0131 344 0414   Fax: 0845 075 6085
E-mail: info@lang-syne.co.uk
www.langsyneshop.co.uk

Design by Dorothy Meikle
Printed by Printwell Ltd
© Lang Syne Publishers Ltd 2019

ISBN 978-1-85217-418-7

Cook

MOTTO:
He shows the safe way
(or) He leads the way.

CREST:
A demi-lion rampant
with a golden ducal coronet.

NAME variations include:
Cooke
Cooks

Echoes of a far distant past
can still be found in most names

Chapter one:

Origins of Scottish surnames

by George Forbes

It all began with the Normans.

For it was they who introduced surnames into common usage more than a thousand years ago, initially based on the title of their estates, local villages and chateaux in France to distinguish and identify these landholdings, usually acquired at the point of a bloodstained sword.

Such grand descriptions also helped enhance the prestige of these arrogant warlords and generally glorify their lofty positions high above the humble serfs slaving away below in the pecking order who only had single names, often with Biblical connotations as in Pierre and Jacques.

The only descriptive distinctions among this peasantry concerned their occupations, like Pierre the swineherd or Jacques the ferryman.

The Normans themselves were originally Vikings (or Northmen) who raided, colonised and eventually settled down around the French coastline.

They had sailed up the Seine in their longboats in 900 AD under their ferocious leader Rollo and ruled the roost in north east France before sailing over to conquer England, bringing their relatively new tradition of having surnames with them.

It took another hundred years for the Normans to percolate northwards and surnames did not begin to appear in Scotland until the thirteenth century.

These adventurous knights brought an aura of chivalry with them and it was said no damsel of any distinction would marry a man unless he had at least two names.

The family names included that of Scotland's great hero Robert De Brus and his compatriots were warriors from families like the De Morevils, De Umphravils, De Berkelais, De Quincis, De Viponts and De Vaux.

As the knights settled the boundaries of their vast estates, they took territorial names, as in Hamilton, Moray, Crawford, Cunningham, Dunbar, Ross, Wemyss, Dundas, Galloway, Renfrew, Greenhill, Hazelwood, Sandylands and Church-hill.

Other names, though not with any obvious geographical or topographical features, nevertheless derived from ancient parishes like Douglas, Forbes, Dalyell and Guthrie.

Other surnames were coined in connection with occupations, castles or legendary deeds. Stuart originated in the word steward, a prestigious post which was an integral part of any large medieval household. The same applied to Cooks, Chamberlains, Constables and Porters.

Borders towns and forts – needed in areas like the Debateable Lands which were constantly fought over by feuding local families – had their own distinctive names; and it was often from them that the resident groups took their communal titles, as in the Grahams of Annandale, the Elliots and Armstrongs of the East Marches, the Scotts and Kerrs of Teviotdale and Eskdale.

Even physical attributes crept into surnames, as in Small, Little and More (the latter being 'beg' in Gaelic), Long or Lang, Stark, Stout, Strong or Strang and even Jolly.

Mieklejohns would have had the strength of several men, while Littlejohn was named after the legendary sidekick of Robin Hood.

Colours got into the act with Black, White, Grey, Brown and Green (Red developed into Reid,

Ruddy or Ruddiman). Blue was rare and nobody ever wanted to be associated with yellow.

Pompous worthies took the name Wiseman, Goodman and Goodall.

Words intimating the sons of leading figures were soon affiliated into the language as in Johnson, Adamson, Richardson and Thomson, while the Norman equivalent of Fitz (from the French-Latin 'filius' meaning 'son') cropped up in Fitzmaurice and Fitzgerald.

The prefix 'Mac' was 'son of' in Gaelic and clans often originated with occupations – as in MacNab being sons of the Abbot, MacPherson and MacVicar being sons of the minister and MacIntosh being sons of the chief.

The church's influence could be found in the names Kirk, Clerk, Clarke, Bishop, Friar and Monk. Proctor came from a church official, Singer and Sangster from choristers, Gilchrist and Gillies from Christ's servant, Mitchell, Gilmory and Gilmour from servants of St Michael and Mary, Malcolm from a servant of Columba and Gillespie from a bishop's servant.

The rudimentary medical profession was represented by Barber (a trade which also once included dentistry and surgery) as well as Leech or Leitch.

Businessmen produced Merchants, Mercers, Monypennies, Chapmans, Sellers and Scales, while down at the old village watermill the names that cropped up included Miller, Walker and Fuller.

Other self explanatory trades included Coopers, Brands, Barkers, Tanners, Skinners, Brewsters and Brewers, Tailors, Saddlers, Wrights, Cartwrights, Smiths, Harpers, Joiners, Sawyers, Masons and Plumbers.

Even the scenery was utilised as in Craig, Moor, Hill, Glen, Wood and Forrest.

Rank, whether high or low, took its place with Laird, Barron, Knight, Tennant, Farmer, Husband, Granger, Grieve, Shepherd, Shearer and Fletcher.

The hunt and the chase supplied Hunter, Falconer, Fowler, Fox, Forrester, Archer and Spearman.

The renowned medieval historian Froissart, who eulogised about the romantic deeds of chivalry (and who condemned Scotland as being a poverty stricken wasteland), once sniffily dismissed the peasantry of his native France as the jacquerie (or the jacques-without-names) but it was these same humble folk who ended up overthrowing the arrogant aristocracy.

In the olden days, only the blueblooded knights of antiquity were entitled to full, proper names, both Christian and surnames, but with the passing of time and a more egalitarian, less feudal atmosphere, more respectful and worthy titles spread throughout the populace as a whole.

Echoes of a far distant past can still be found in most names and they can be borne with pride in commemoration of past generations who fought and toiled in some capacity or other to make our nation what it now is, for good or ill.

Chapter two:

King and Covenant

Ranked at 83 in the list of the top 100 surnames in Scotland and also popular throughout the rest of the United Kingdom and much further afield, 'Cook' and its popular variant of 'Cooke' is an occupational surname denoting someone who worked as a cook or worked in a place where cooked food was served.

Thought to have derived from the Anglo-Saxon 'coc', or 'cocus', the first record of the name is found in the English region of Essex in the middle of the twelfth century.

Also prevalent throughout Scotland from earliest times, it is recorded how a Richard Cocus was a witness to a charter in 1260 while, in what is now the equally redundant form of 'Kuk', an Andro Kuk is recorded as having been banished from Dundee in 1521 for having offended the Church authorities.

The name also came from Scotland to Ireland through what was known as 'plantation' – a policy that involved the settlement of loyal Protestants on the island throughout the reigns of England's Elizabeth I, James I (James VI of Scotland) and Charles I.

The vast majority of 'transplanted' Scottish bearers of the Cook name settled in the northern province of Ulster, where place names to this day include Cooksland and Cookstown.

Another source of the name on the Emerald Isle is from the original native Irish MacDhadhocs, a branch of the powerful Burkes of the ancient province of Connacht.

In common with the bearers of many other occupational surnames, not all bearers of the Cook name necessarily followed the trade that the name indicates.

While, for example, Clan Stewart of Appin would indeed have had need of 'cooks' within their community, not all bearers of the Cook name were actually so employed.

Recognised by some sources as a sept, or sub-branch, of this proud West Highland clan, along with others who include the Cruickshanks, MacCloys, Moodies and Sharps, the Cooks would have more likely been found on the bloody field of battle rather in the domestic environment of the kitchen.

As a sept of this clan, whose motto is "Whither will ye" and crest a unicorn's head, the Cooks shared in both its glorious fortunes and tragic misfortunes – and, accordingly, are entitled to share in honours that include the wearing of the clan tartan.

With their territory located between Ballachulish, on the south shore of Loch Leven, and Benderloch, and ruling from their ancient but now ruined seat of Castle Stalker, their territorial name survives on the landscape to this day in the form of Port Appin.

They are also known as "The Loyal Clan", because of their devotion to the cause of the Royal House of Stewart – a bond that ultimately led to tragedy.

Attainted for treason for their support of James III in the Rising of 1715, nearly 100 of their clansmen and kinsfolk fell on the field of Culloden just over 30 years later.

This was in support of the equally ill-fated Rising led by Charles Edward Stewart, better known to posterity as Bonnie Prince Charlie.

Lowland Scottish bearers of the name had meanwhile earlier been prominent in the Covenanting movement.

A National Covenant, pledging defence of

the Presbyterian religion, was signed in the Greyfriars Kirk, in Edinburgh, in February of 1638.

Copies were circulated throughout Scotland, and the hundreds of ordinary men and women who subscribed to it became known as Covenanters.

Following the restoration to the throne of Charles II in 1660, the death knell for the Covenanting movement was sounded when a Recissory Act was passed, declaring the Covenant illegal.

Episcopal rule was foisted on the Scottish Church, and all ministers who refused to adhere to this new order were deprived of their parishes.

Persecuted by the forces of authority, the Covenanters rose in futile rebellion in November of 1666 and, as a sign of the harsh treatment that was to be subsequently meted out to them, many of the prisoners taken were tortured and hanged.

A Covenanting victory was achieved at the battle of Drumclog in June of 1679, only to be followed a few short weeks later by resounding defeat at the battle of Bothwell Brig, near Hamilton, when nearly 800 Covenanters were killed and 1,400 taken prisoner.

Kept for several weeks in open cages in Greyfriars Kirkyard, prisoners who agreed to sign a bond for future 'good behaviour' were released, but by November of 1679 more than 250 steadfastly recalcitrant prisoners still remained.

These included an Andrew Cook, from the Borders town of Melrose.

The authorities decided to sell them as slaves on the steaming plantations of Barbados, and arrangements were accordingly made to transport them there aboard the *Crown of London*.

But the vessel foundered on December 10th off the headland of Scarva Taing, near the Mull Head of Deerness, in Orkney, during a violent storm, and an estimated 209 prisoners, including Andrew Cook, were drowned while still locked below decks.

The period 1680 to 1685 was known as "The Killing Time", and one of the many victims of this particularly brutal period was the Lanarkshire Covenanter and weaver Thomas Cook.

Seized by Government troops and interrogated over his allegiances, he refused to give a straight-forward answer as to whether or not he was willing to pray for the King.

He was summarily shot dead on the spot, along with two others who had also been seized and similarly questioned.

His body now rests in Old Cathcart Kirkyard.

Chapter three:

Exploration and politics

Bearers of the Cook name have stamped their mark on the historical record through a number of intrepid endeavours.

Not the least of these was the sea captain, navigator, cartographer and explorer James Cook, born in 1728 in the village of Marton, Yorkshire.

The second of eight children of James Cook, a farm labourer who had left his native Scotland and settled in Marton, marrying local girl Grace Pace, he was aged only about 13 when he joined the Merchant Navy, enlisting in the Royal Navy two years later.

Seeing action in North America in the Seven Years War with France from 1756 to 1763, he not only mapped the entrances to the St Lawrence River during the Siege of Quebec, but also was later responsible for making the first highly detailed map of Newfoundland.

In 1766, in command of *Endeavour*, he made the first of three Pacific voyages that resulted in the first recorded circumnavigation of New Zealand and the first European contact with Australia's eastern coastline and the Hawaiian Islands.

It was on his third Pacific voyage, in command of *Resolution* that, in February of 1779, and through a misunderstanding, Hawaiian islanders killed him.

The islanders, treating his body with respect, accorded him full funerary honours according to their own customs, later returning it to the British for burial at sea.

The site where he was killed on Hawaii, at Kealakekua Bay, is now marked with an obelisk, while he is also remembered through not only giving his name to the Cook Islands, Cook Strait and Cook Inlet, but also in more recent times through the Moon crater Cook.

No less intrepid than Captain Cook, but decidedly more controversial, was Frederick Cook, born in 1865 in Sullivan County, New York.

While no doubt can be cast on some of his accomplishments, doubts remain to this day over some of his claimed feats.

These are, in particular, his claims that he was the first to ascend Mount McKinley and also that he reached the North Pole before his fellow American rival Robert Peary.

Qualifying as a medical doctor in 1890, he was appointed surgeon for Peary's Arctic expedition of 1891 to 1892, while he also served as surgeon on the Belgian Antarctic Expedition of 1897 to 1899.

This was an expedition that also involved the famed Norwegian explorer Roald Amundsen, and what is beyond any doubt is that Cook played a vital role in helping to save the lives of the expedition when their ship, *Belgica*, was held ice-bound for several weeks in the merciless grip of an Antarctic winter.

In 1903, Cook led the first expedition to Mount McKinley, Alaska, followed by another expedition three years later in which he claimed to have been the first to ascend to its summit.

Unfortunately, however, his detailed records of this expedition to the highest point in North America were lost, while a photograph of Cook on one of the mountain's peaks was later claimed to be a fake.

This allegation was made following his claimed feat of having reached the North Pole in April of 1908, a year before his rival Peary achieved the goal.

Claim and counter-claim abounded that Cook had faked photographic records of his trek to the Pole – although no firm evidence has ever been produced that he actually did so.

His reputation received a further blow in 1923 when, after having entered the Texas oil business, he was imprisoned after having been found guilty of attempting to defraud potential investors by exaggerating the extent of an oil find.

It was not until after his release from prison in 1930 that it transpired he had been wrongly convicted.

Granted a pardon by Franklin D. Roosevelt in 1940 in a belated attempt to restore Cook's much-tarnished reputation, he died only a few weeks later.

Not an explorer himself, but someone who started a business more than 170 years ago that allows others to explore the world, Thomas Cook was a founder of what thrives to this day as the Thomas Cook Group.

While travellers of today may, should they wish, partake of alcoholic refreshment on their Thomas Cook travels, this was certainly not the case when the company was founded.

Born in 1808 in Melbourne, Derbyshire, Cook was a strict adherent of the Baptist faith and, foreswearing the consumption of alcohol, was a prominent member of the Temperance Society, whose members took a solemn pledge never to let alcohol pass their lips.

In 1841, and by this time a Baptist preacher, Cook chartered a train to take 570 Temperance campaigners from Leicester to a rally in Loughborough, only eleven miles away.

This trip proved so successful that, later joined by John Mason Cook, who only by coincidence had the same surname, he established a business that ran rail excursions throughout the United Kingdom.

By 1845, and no longer restricted to Temperance Society members, the enterprise had flourished to such an extent that the Thomas Cook Company was offering highly popular tours of Europe, while by the 1860s it was taking travellers to as far afield as Egypt.

In 1874, for the benefit of travellers faced with the problem of dealing with numerous international currencies, the company introduced 'circular notes' – later developed by American Express as the 'traveller's cheques' that we know today.

The company remained in the hands of the Cook family until 1928, thirty-six years after Thomas

Cook's death, and has gone through numerous owners ever since – but still retains the proud Cook name.

From exploration and travel to the often cut-throat world of politics, bearers of the Cook name have also earned their place in the historical record.

In common with Thomas Cook, Arthur James Cook, better known as A.J. Cook, was also a Baptist preacher – but it was in the sphere of political activism, rather than travel, that he made his name.

Born in 1883 in Wookey, Somerset, he moved to South Wales at the age of 18 to find work in the coalmines.

Fired by his Baptist zeal and his dedication to the improvement of the condition of the working class, he became a member of the Independent Labour Party (ILP) and, through his opposition to Britain's involvement in the First World War, was sentenced to three months imprisonment in 1918 for sedition.

General Secretary of the Miners' Federation of Great Britain from 1924 to 1931 – a period that included the General Strike of 1926 – he became famous for his rallying cry of "Not a penny off the pay, not a second on the day."

Also a secretary of the International Miners' Federation, he died in 1931.

Also having toiled as a coal miner before gaining prominence in the world of politics, Sir Joseph Cook rose from humble beginnings to become 6th Prime Minister of Australia.

Born in 1860 in Silverdale, Staffordshire, and beginning work in the mines at the age of only nine, he immigrated in the 1880s to Lithgow, New South Wales.

Taking up employment in the mines and championing the cause of fellow workers, he became General Secretary of the Western Miners' Association in 1887 and a founding member four years later of the Australian Labor Party.

When elected in 1891 to the New South Wales Legislative Assembly as Member for Hartley, he also became the first to be elected to a Labor seat in the Australian Parliament.

In what were the complex Australian party political allegiances of the time, he later switched from the Labor Party to the Free Trade Party and, later again, to the Commonwealth Liberal Party.

It was as leader of this party that he served from June of 1913 to September of 1914 as 6th Prime Minister of Australia.

He died in 1947, after having earlier received

the honour of knighthood, while in 1972 he was also honoured through an Australian postage stamp.

From Australia and back to one of the Cook homelands of Scotland, Robin Cook was the leading Labour Party politician who was born in 1946 in Bellshill, Lanarkshire.

Following a period as a school teacher after having studied English literature at Edinburgh University, he entered politics to serve, between 1974 and 1983, as Labour Member of Parliament (MP) for Edinburgh Central and, from 1983 until his death in 2005, as MP for Livingston.

Recognised as having been one of the greatest political debaters of his time, his high government offices included, from 1997 to 2001, Foreign Secretary and Leader of the House of Commons – a post from which he dramatically resigned in March of 2003 in protest over the invasion of Iraq.

Chapter four:

On the world stage

Bearers of the Cook and Cooke names have gained international fame through pursuits ranging from acting and music to sport and invention.

Born in San Francisco in 1903, **Elisha Cook Jr.** was the veteran American character actor who, in the role of Wilmer, played beside Humphrey Bogart in the 1941 *The Maltese Falcon*.

Starting in vaudeville at the age of 14, other memorable films in which he appeared include *The Big Sleep*, from 1946, the 1959 *Baby Face Nelson*, and, from 1968, *Rosemary's Baby*; he died in 1995.

Born in London in 1906, **Beryl Cooke** was the popular British actress of television and film who starred as Aunt Lucy in the BBC sitcom *Happy Ever After* and as Mrs Vance in the BBC drama *Tenko*.

She died in 2001, after having also appeared in films that include the 1954 *Conflict of Wings* and, from 1971, *She'll Follow You Anywhere*.

On the stage, **Barbara Cook**, born in 1927 in Atlanta, Georgia, is the American actress and singer who, in 1956, starred in the Broadway musical

Candide and the 1957 *The Music Man*, for which she won a Tony Award.

Her Broadway show *A Concert for the Theatre* won her a Drama Desk Award in 1987, while ten years later she celebrated her 70th birthday by giving a performance at London's Albert Hall with the Royal Philharmonic Orchestra

Recognised as one of the pioneers in Britain of 'anti-establishment comedy', **Peter Cook** was the comedian, writer and satirist who was born in 1937 in Torquay, Devon.

It was in 1961 that he opened the comedy venue The Establishment Club in London's Soho, while a year later he was one of the stars of BBC Television's satirical current affairs programme *That Was The Week That Was*.

His comedy partnership with the late Dudley Moore led to the *Not Only … But Also …* television show, while he also provided financial backing for the satirical magazine *Private Eye*; he died in 1995.

Born in 1972 in Boston, **Dane Cook** is the American stand-up comedian and film actor whose best-selling albums of his comedy routines include *Harmful if Swallowed* and *Retaliation*, and who has also appeared in films that include the 1999 *Mystery Men* and the 2008 *My Best Friend's Girl*.

One particularly distinguished bearer of the name in the world of broadcasting and journalism was **Alistair Cooke**, who was born of Anglo-Irish stock in 1908 in Salford, Lancashire.

Settling in the United States in 1937 and taking up U.S. citizenship four years later, he subsequently became famous for his BBC radio series *Letter from America*, while in 1952 he became the host of *Omnibus* – the first commercial television series in America dedicated to the arts.

Also known for his much acclaimed 1973 13-part television series *America: A Personal History of the United States*, he died in 2004 at the age of 95 – the recipient of numerous honours and awards that include an honorary knighthood for his outstanding contribution to Anglo-American understanding.

In contemporary music, Quentin Leo Cook, also known as Norman Cook, but much better known as **Fatboy Slim**, is the English DJ, 'big beat' musician and record producer recognised as a pioneer of the music genre known as electric dance.

Born in 1963 in Reigate, Surrey, he has achieved a number of chart hits, performing with bands that include The Housemartins, while he also performs under the rather offbeat name of The Brighton Port Authority.

Rising to fame after winning the seventh season of the music talent show *American Idol* in 2007, **David Cook** is the rock singer and songwriter who was born in 1982 in Houston, Texas, and whose best-selling self-titled album was released in 2008.

Also from the seventh season of *American Idol*, country singer **Kristy Lee Cook** was the seventh placed finalist who later enjoyed top music chart success with her single *15 Minutes*.

Recognised as one of the pioneers of soul music and, accordingly, known as the King of Soul, **Sam Cooke** was the gospel, blues, soul and pop singer and songwriter who was born Sam Cook in 1931 in Clarksdale, Mississippi.

One of the first African-American performers to personally handle the business side of his career, he had no less than 29 Top 40 hits in the Unites States between 1957 and 1964, including *You Send Me*, *Chain Gang*, *Wonderful World* and *Bring It on Home to Me*.

His career came to an abrupt and tragic end in December of 1964, at the age of 33, when he was shot dead by the manager of a motel in which he was staying in Los Angles.

The court ruled at the time that he had been 'drunk and distressed' and the manager had killed him in self-defence – although the circumstances surrounding the shooting remain a matter of controversy.

He was inducted into the Rock and Roll Hall of Fame in 1986.

Born in 1945, **Stu Cook** is the bass guitarist and songwriter who, along with Doug Clifford and brothers Tom and John Fogerty, was a member of the American band Creedance Clearwater Revival.

Inducted into the Rock and Roll Hall of Fame in 1993, the band enjoyed hits throughout the late 1960s and early 1970s that include *Run Through the Jungle*, *Up Around the Bend*, *Bad Moon Rising* and *Have You Ever Seen the Rain?*

Born in 1956 in London, **Paul Cook** is the drummer and member of the controversial punk rock band the Sex Pistols, formed in 1975, while Richard Cook, who was better known as **R.D. Cook**, was the noted British jazz writer who was born in 1957 in Kew, Surrey, and who died in 2007.

From music to the equally creative world of art, **Beryl Cook** was the self-taught painter who was aged nearly 50 before the first exhibition of her work was staged.

Born in Plymouth in 1926 as Beryl Tansley, and with Cook her married name, it was not until Bernard Samuels, of the Plymouth Arts Centre, first saw her unique comical paintings of people that he persuaded her in 1975 to hold an exhibition.

This resulted in a cover page feature in the *Sunday Times* magazine, followed a year later by her first exhibition in London.

Awarded an OBE in 1995, the artist, who died in 2008, executed her painting, *The Royal Couple*, for the Queen's Golden Jubilee Exhibition in 2002.

In the green-fingered world of horticulture, **William Cook,** born in 1884 in New Plymouth, Auckland, New Zealand, to Scottish parents, was the founder in 1910 of the Eastwood Hill Arboretum, now the National Arboretum of New Zealand.

'Eastwood Hill' was named after the house on the southern outskirts of Glasgow where his mother, Jessie, had grown up; a Fellow of the Royal New Zealand Institute of Horticulture, he died in 1967.

In the world of the written word, **Michael Cook**, born in 1933 in Fulham, London, and who later settled in Newfoundland, Canada, was the playwright whose noted works include the 1971 *Tiln*, the 1974 *Jacob's Wake* and, written fourteen years before his death in 1994, *The Gayden Chronicles*.

Born in 1929 in Lakemba, New South Wales, **Kenneth Cook** was the Australian journalist, novelist and film director whose best known novel, *Wake in Fright*, was adapted for film in 1971 under the title in the United Sates and Europe of *Outback*.

Also known for his humorous *Killer Koala* trilogy, he died in 1987.

In the realms of science fiction and fantasy, **Glen Cook** is the best-selling American author, born in 1944, known for his *The Black Company* fantasy series and *Garrett P.I.* series of novels.

Born in New York City in 1940, **Dr Robin Cook** is the American physician and novelist whose futuristic medical thrillers include his 1977 *Coma*, the 1997 *Invasion* and, from 2010, *Cure*.

Blending science fiction and fantasy, **Hugh Cook**, born in 1956 in what is now Banaba Island, Kiribati, and who later settled in New Zealand, was the author who achieved cult status with his *The Chronicles of an Age of Darkness* series, written between 1986 and 1992; he died in 2008.

Yet another **Hugh Cook** is the author born in

1942 in The Hague, Amsterdam, and who immigrated with his family to Canada at the age of eight, and whose novels include his 1985 *Cracked Wheat and Other Stories* and the 1998 *Home in Alfalfa*.

Born in 1932 in Chicago, **Bruce Alexander Cook** was the American journalist and author best known for his historical and crime novels that include his 1978 *Sex Life* and the 1992 *Death as a Career Move*; he died in 2003.

Not only a best-selling American mystery writer, **Ann Turner Cook** was also the model for the iconic artwork image still used to this day on baby food packages manufactured by the Gerber Products Company.

Born in 1928, the daughter of syndicated American newspaper columnist Leslie Turner, she was five months old when their neighbour, the artist Dorothy Hope Smith, executed a charcoal drawing of her and submitted it to Gerber.

The company had at the time been looking for a suitable image for its line of baby food products, and Smith's drawing of Ann was accepted.

After retiring from school teaching, the Gerber model turned her talents to full-time writing, and is now the best-selling author of the *Brandy O'Bannon* series of mysteries that include the 2001 *Trace their Shadows* and the 2008 *Micanopy in Shadow*.

Bearers of the Cook name have also excelled in the highly competitive world of sport.

Born in 1955 in Lansing, Michigan, **Alice Cook** is the American skater who, along with partner William Fauver, won the silver medal for pair skating at the 1976 Olympics.

Born in 1975 in Townsville, Queensland, **Natalie Cook** is the Australian professional beach volleyball player who, along with partner Kerri Pottharst, won the gold medal for the sport at the 2000 Olympics.

In cricket, **Alastair Cook**, born in 1984 in Gloucester, is the English international left-handed opening batsman who has played county cricket for Essex.

One particularly inventive bearer of the name was **William Fothergill Cooke**, born near London in 1806 and who died in 1879.

Along with Charles Wheatstone, he was the co-inventor of the Cooke-Wheatstone electrical telegraph, while he was also the co-founder in 1846, along with John Lewis Ricardo, of the Electric Telegraph Company – the world's first public telegraph company.